Beyond Reflections!

Reflections ++

ILA SINGH

BookLeaf Publishing

India | USA | UK

Made with ❤ on the BookLeaf Publishing Platform

www.bookleafpub.in

www.bookleafpub.com

Dedication

It's my privilege and honor to dedicate this second free verse book titled 'Beyond Reflections' to the curious readers who are also the seekers here on earth school; seekers are invariably enthusiastic about life in general and 'Self' in particular, aspiring to be the best version of themselves in 2025 and beyond.

Preface

Beyond Reflections is definitely more specific and focused from Reflections!; hence I fondly refer to it as Reflections ++. During course of unlearning, we may come across certain gaps, which may be difficult to ignore; but they can be addressed effectively by adopting a 'zero- thought mindset', with inbuilt pauses (conscious or unconscious): providing sufficient opportunity to become more meaningful and holistic. The idea is to explore the 'unknown' mindfully, so as to seize them, with adequate time and space; to be a silent observer transmuting the hidden 'unknown' gradually to the 'known' within.

Acknowledgements

I am deeply grateful to all the readers on earth school; who accept, acknowledge and value the presence of ideas, views and observations under 'Beyond Reflections' and it's relevance in life. They are enthusiastic to connect to the finer details, to admire and appreciate the miracles that show up for each one of us at appropriate time and space.

1. Wander with Wonder

As the mind wanders, the feet start to explore,
chasing the Sun till dusk, chilling in moonlight to snore,
in every step, a new and unique story unfolds in store,
Wander free in curiosity to feel more,
with a wonder-filled default backend program at core,
Wonder where streets are new, and people adore.

The Kingdom of Nature, where deep forests reside,
I wander in wonder, with a wonderful advise,
swaying branches, rustling leaves, the crispy breeze,
echoes of magic flows, as the glow worms greets,
Mind used to wander, is now in the state to seize.

Despite the twilight, the eyes can see beyond the chore,
where harmony rests, as symphony a graceful core,
the waves of wander arise, to delight the shore,
I am swept away in amaze, with invisible secrets galore,
as a Kaleidoscope of diverse patterns, to score.

Wandering at safe pace, to capture dawn's golden rays,

diversity bustling, as silence awaits always,
curiosity as a compass wanders, where liberty stays,
the wandering waves pause, at wonder-filled bays,
All creatures great and small, Wander with Wonder in
maze!

2. Vicious Cycle

In the depths within, an invisible cycle reside,
a mixed bag of pain, fear and doubts to hide,
a never ending loop, the freedom of choice wide,
the cycle is tough to ride, with a black hole inside,
a little birdie in cage, wanting to escape this ride.

In this invisible net, issues are entangled or trapped,
A whirlpool of events, where circumstances are
wrapped,
the chaos where people, places and things are strapped,
a door to unlock, a code to crack, a puzzle sapped,
this cycle keeps spinning, with a 360 view mapped.

The idea is to break free and discover foresight,
shatter the chains, to unlock closed doors upright,
to find the light, that guides across the dark night,
discover the courage, to break the cycles might,
rise like a phoenix, from the ashes of past fright.

In these endless loops, the opportunities mingle,

with a choice to make, a chance to take and tingle,
working on strength, to assemble and jingle,
confidence to overtake this illusionary dingle,
in time and space, overcome the threats and twinkle.

Yes, it's all about motion, without any escape,
Like a hamster on wheel, with a quest to frape,
Fleeting dreams, floating vision, creating new landscape,
Vicious wheel keeps spinning, effortlessly to generate,
Absorbed, procrastinate, ruminate without any solace.

In this vortex, I find my courage, my place,
a spiral staircase, a rabbit hole to displace,
the pace is involving, both wild and free to face,
unstoppable, unlimited version, in space,
a source of inspiration, to Go Forth as human race.

To renew and resurrect, is only a choice,
let's break free to decode the voice,
the Centre Stage is ready, with appropriate poise,
letting go of perceived darkness and noise,
with sincere efforts, the cocoon cracks and dries,
the chrysalis emerges, in bright wings flies. .

Acknowledge, sharpen and acquire new skills,
to let the invisible, irresistible force, reflect as a frill,
tap in creative pursuits, step-by-step as a drill,

embrace the spin, to emerge stronger, wiser and chill,
Vicious cycle spins to teach freedom is the thrill!!

3. Overcome

Beneath the silent struggle, flame of resilience thrive,
simmering in robust frame, learning to bend and survive,
where shadows dissolve, in the potential to rise,
a new assurance unfolds, in acceptance to strive,
no 'if's' or 'but's'; only focused awareness to derive.

The voice of doubt whispers, to ignite the fear,
an insecure, unknown critique resides here,
sounds familiar, to be good enough dear,
draw on the wisdom and know what to bear,
find abundant trust and faith within so clear.

For every peak conquered, a new peak appears,
a new challenge to overcome, to wipe off all tears,
Slowly but steadily, learn to overtake with care,
A testament to courage, mental strength so rare,
Take a pledge over illusionary obstacles and dare,
Seize the moment of learning, that is here.

Yes, we are all broken, shattered and torn,

yet their is enough wisdom, to reborn,
have been tested, tried and withdrawn,
yet, have refused to give in, to let the spirits worn,
this is the time to weed out all the thorn,
to willfully acknowledge, wipe off all that's gone.

I am unbroken and unbowed, yet not afraid,
to overcome the hurdles, and not be enslaved,
As a phoenix, arising to upgrade,
in this sacred space to pervade,
Shadows lose their grip, as light of hope parade,
Overcome!! to arise over and over again!!

.

4. Hope

A force within, stops to enquire,
as breath nurtures the spark, to fuel the fire,
an anchor to hold, a future to desire,
amidst the turmoil, emotions rage and aspire,
a gentle whisper, to calm down and inquire
a promise that echo's, better days to admire.

A bridge spans across the promised land,
where eternal flame ignites the brand,
like a north star, navigate to stand,
surfing the turbulent rough sea grand,
a trendy flame of care and trust bland,
where hope a trusted gift, unwraps strands.

In the garden of mind, thoughts bloom to shine,
like the fresh air of spring, all the senses rhyme,
a delicate scent of promise to design,
draws to the beauty hidden within and align,
a shining beacon, to dispel doubts benign,
Hope as a sun shine, guides to the divine.

Hope a double-edged sword, cuts through despair,
creating a future, overlooking the past to dare,
on one hand, hope reflects a promising future to flare,
meanwhile, on other hand, to mourn the losses we bear,
this duality is a mystery to realize here,
where contradiction is only a story to share.

Hope, a delicate flower, blooms in cracks at broken hour,
a beauty divine, fragile like a withering flower,
a gentle whisper, shining like a morning shower,
flickering options, like flames to brighten the tower,
morning promises ensures, difficulties are over,
Hope's horizon stretches wide to conquer and takeover.

5. Knowledge Vs Wisdom

Knowledge a treasure, of facts, figures, vast and wide,
acquired through degrees, diplomas, a recognition by
side,
a tool to give power and sharpen the skill beside,
a collection of data, relevant and useful information to
guide,
Knowledge fills the mind, like a mountain's pride.

Wisdom a compass true, a key to unlock door,
wisdom's way is neither a recognition, nor a destination
to bore,
It's a journey of acceptance, understanding and so much
more,
listen to the wisdom's whisper; the voice at core,
in the maze of life, a gentler pace to score.

In the garden of life, there is a magnificent tree to
admire,
this Tree of Knowledge bears leaves to perspire,
branches stretch gracefully, as roots dive in deep spire,

Tree of Knowledge is an amazing site, for vibrant bloom
desire,
shade of wisdom is the respite, that juicy fruit require. .

Knowledge and Wisdom, are sides of the same coin right,
One without the other, is like savory without delight,
Knowledge provides foresight, as wisdom is the insight,
'balance of knowledge', in coherence with 'wisdom's
might',
invites all individuals to share space with the knight.

Path of knowledge, a journey of sharp, smart, brilliant
mind,
a quest for reasoning, that's driven by curiosity and
grind,
while the path of wisdom, a choice to unfold,
a quest for meaning, that alters the untold,
Knowledge empowers, enriches the domain of science to
hold,
Wisdom is in observing, acknowledging the threshold.

Reflections is not just about all that we know,
but how we respond, to capture all that we don't know,
Knowledge a dependable robust foundation to grace,
in adequate time and space, the wisdom grows at its
pace,

the chapters about different phases of life grace,
to merge the power of Knowledge with Wisdom's ace.

12

6. Transformation aka Transmutation

Caterpillar's mindless consumption ends,
as the challenge to carry it's weight bends,
eventually giving up on the routine trend,
to pause, absorb, instigate and attend,
wrapping itself in stillness to blend,
give up on munching, to let nature amend.

Cooperating, coordinating, releasing all resistance,
while adopting the new cocoon phase assistance,
the world outside seizes to attract any distance,
in this new dark unknown stage of existence,
initial hesitation, yet to adapt the change insistence,
the pupa is transforming to commemorate persistence.

The cocoon cracks, making way for chrysalis to peep,
unfolding wings, unfurling, stretching, searching deep,
to reach for a new form in spring and leap,
it's neither the same caterpillar nor pupa to creep,
this is a new form for the butterfly to own and keep,

a choice of freedom, to soar or weep.

Dark coal under high pressure, transforms to sparkling
diamond,
transformation a process, to burn the old, opt for a new
bound,
Transformation releases the chains of past, for creation
to sound,
the journey of transformation is not easy to get around,
assurance for renewal from the old phase found,
Transformation aka Transmutation is to astound.

7. Celebrations!!

In the mental garden of happiness, flowers bloom and
thrive,
creating space for laughter echoes, where fountain of joy
reside,
this feeling is contagious, as a scent so fine,
creating new melodies, a new vision to be alive,
in this harmony of vibrations, where symphony jive,
Celebration as a choice, is for us to strive.

Life as a canvas, where vibrant colors blend and
submerge,
A tapestry of moments, eager to cherish and emerge,
a mixed bag of experiences, where potpourri of
memories merge,
though a fleeting state, yet energizing to splurge,
an amalgam of love, joy, fears and doubts surge,
a decision to facilitate this genuine urge.

On a route that is exciting, a ride that is exhilarating,
a mystery unfolding, a new story decoding,

to dance with sun shine, to sing in rain,
Joy a trusted companion, overtakes all sufferings and
pain,
Usually a choice to make, a chance to take yet again,
Idea is to know the game, a gesture to gain,
Celebration a sense of contentment to fame.

Happiness, the elixir of life overflows, smile a universal
language to explore,
in this contagious state, where imaginations are galore,
as 'Carrier of Light', as 'Warrior of Choice', difficult to
ignore,
as' Master of Celebrations', as 'Change Makers' and
'Game Changer',
this treasured time, to feel the delight and share,
Live life 'King Size', where Celebrations flare.

8. Joy of Healing

Under the depths of each being, a silent wound reside,
a hurt that is hidden, yet denied,
in the shadows of persona, it lingered and stayed,
a constant reminder of it's existence, yet never claimed,
focus often to dive in deep, a little deeper to frame,
each aware breath, connects to feel this dull, known
pain.

This discovery was not easy, as it is an emotional
bondage,
I learned to be compassionate to 'self', to nurture and rise
again,
the 'little me' till date was scared, about the past misery
of despair,
assuring this 'little child', the toughest litmus test,
with adequate mental strength, trace the scars crest,
gradually the forces align, to create the best.

The journey of inner healing, is the one we take alone,
it requires abundant patience, courage, and willingness

to adobe,
rewards are unlimited, to wipe every tear out,
keep moving, one step at a time, without doubt,
healing is appealing, with self worth profound,
richness of wellness overflows, with wholeness all
around.

No doctor, no pharmacy, no clinic can heal our self,,
as the power of healing resides within thyself,
an inner wisdom, that knows, exactly where to shelf,
the choicest voice of intuition, that shouts at oneself,
no external remedy, can replace this inner elf,
as the power of healing certainly overtake the self.

The doctors diagnose, to only cut and paste,
while the pharmacy may prescribe and wait,
true healing comes with self's inner sight,
to take the ownership of the health alright,
Body Temple's wisdom, whispers truth to enlight,
where meditation as medicine unfolds so bright.

Health as the only true wealth to treasure,
its not just physical, but mental and emotional pressure,
a sense of well being, is essential to feel better,
investing in healing, is yielding more to ether,
wealth of self-care, a precious insurance forever,

let's prioritize this wealth, to invest in health wherever,
to reap the rewards as Joy of Healing together.

. Annealing

In the heart of furnace, flames dance, flicker and sway,
fire of resilience, making space, day by day,
this fire is pure energy, churning past away,
leaving metal strong and flexible, for future today,
high temperature and pressure, melts all in dismay,
the rigid gets malleable, mild and ductile to stay.

Fire of annealing is unique, to let go of all rigidity, and
flow,
revealing the purity, in gentleness or either break with
blow,
gradually as the metal cools, in a new form to settle and
glow,
a new pattern, a new shape, emerges to hold tight and
show,
the fire of annealing, is simply a true metaphor for life to
grow,
transforming raw metal to gold, where mercury as
bridge to know.

Just as the raw metal is heated, and modified by the
flame,
Humans also change by the trials and sufferings they
face,
the power of annealing, an impactful ancient art in place,
where raw human awareness, transmutes to formulate,
to renew, refresh, rejuvenate, resurrect in phase,
as a calm, composed, blissful Being in grace.

This fire of annealing, is essential for spiritual respite,
purification fire burns, all insecurities, doubt and fears
alike,
the crucible of everyday chores, depletes the precious life
energy and more,
carefully refining various levels, clears all impurities to
shore,
in this alchemical process, annealing as a catalyst prime,
transmutes raw iron into lustrous bright gold to shine.

Weaning from the past, releases memories to hold us
fast,
softening of edges, blurring of lines to cast,
to wean ourselves, from the comfort zone aghast,
familiar habits, patterns, and feelings resolves clast,
like a piece of clay, molded and shaped in blast,
Duality dissolves, Annealing a spot light to last.

10. Trust and believe to achieve!

A key to unlock the dreams that reside,
a robust foundation that's true and fine,
acknowledge the moments that make us alive,
a sheer calmness, that the world can't realize,
Know your self worth, to be wild and free,
trust the instincts and ideas to be me.

As a Creative Director of life,
in wonder and might, soar on wings of inner glee,
Trust the voice, where belief reside,
in the depths of silence, let the timid voice arise,
this path of faith, an exclusive way to divine,
Trust yourself dear one, to let your spirit guide.

Faith as the purpose, invites every time,
as a dependable support, surfing across the ebb and tide,
with a secure knowing, let's navigate the unknown and refine,
as robust faith in intentions, hold the sail as shrine,

believe to trust, that's unwavering as mysteries line,
a bond that's unbreakable, through the darkest night
fine.

Leap of trust is necessary, to know the risks to take,
Vision is unknown, Mission unspun to create,
the labyrinth of trust, a bond to commemorate,
a believe that is unshakable, in the maze of mind to fake,
roots of self-trust are deep, to nourish and celebrate,
Trust and believe to achieve the desired fate!!

11. Tranquility

The stillness of dawn, as the world is yet to awake,
a transient, impermanent sense, that only nature can
create,
sound of dry leaves rustling, reorganizing to form a lane,
branches sway, spreading the delicate scent sane,
shades of sky are vibrant, a perfect ambience to create,
refreshed senses arise, making the world rejuvinate.

In between the gaps, I find my peaceful nest,
a place where anxiety fades, as the mind finds space to
rest,
despite yesterdays chaos, and tomorrow's test,
the playful river flows, over, under and around the rock's
crest,
the chirping birds sing a new song in delight,
to welcome and cheer the dependable Sun light.

A refuge, a sanctuary from the storm, a place to align
and meditate,
the path is rough, winding and slow, yet the choice is

profound to state,
this is certainly a unique, unusual road, for courage as
cape to emulate,
walking on this path, I find my inner wisdom to
speculate,
a robust support, a sense of belonging in serenity to
commemorate,
this inner compass, is the refuge from storms to
instigate.

In midst of all chaos, I can now find my space, an oasis to
stay,
to recharge, to reflect, to release, all the chores of the
day,
as the calm surface of the mighty ocean, to reflect and
play,
a joy in coherence with awesome cosmic view say,
gentle ripples glides across the mind to 'zero thought'
bay,
dissolving all the fear, in stillness along the way,
the serene reflections as balm, wipes out all the tears
today,
in this quite place, I find my unique Tranquil sway!

12. Synchronicity

In the web of everyday life, threads intersect, entangle to
refine,
this illusionary construct, a maze of intrinsic, attractive
profile,
meaningful coincidences, a cosmic rhyme, a symphony
so fine,
the magical connections between people, places and
events chime,
as the spider web of relationships, transcends the
ordinary rhyme,
in the realm of circumstances, a complex interplay
entwine.

Jumbled up values, potpourri of issues, in a pandora box
is undefine,
Universal laws exist, within the sublime, to understand
and shine,
a quest for wonder, an awe-inspiring moment, assuring
there is more to life,
this awesome creator, our guide, provides abundant

opportunities to define,
a connection that spans the gap, between the known and
unknown divine,
Synchronicity as a bridge, seamlessly connects the inner
and outer world prime.

A Cosmic dance, where all stars, milky ways and planets
phase,
A 'Tandav' of celestial bodies, creating harmony to
phrase,
It's all Centre Stage, so magnificent and in grace,
the Universal Master Plan, with concealed symbols to
trace,
Providing base where we are interlocked in space,
Individual's life, as part of the 'Chakravyu', as intricate
chase.

Experiences of life, its unique patterns, woven with care
for all to reside,
our exclusive stories, as part of narrative unfolds, for us
to decide,
a riddle awaiting individual's attention, that is rare to
strike,
as mystery unfolds, unraveled, is full of surprise,
the ancient secrets remain untold, uncalled for twists to
arise,

as labyrinth of life awaiting, to unveil the Synchronicity
to sublime.

28

13. Heartfulness!!

With every breath, let the awareness expand,
to attempt a connection, with all creatures on land,
a perception wrapped in empathy, and kindness to blend,
an effortless fountain of compassion, that has no end,
in this state of heartfulness, I am free to amend,
the best version of myself, that's genuine and authentic
trend.

A heart that's full of gratitude and kindness to be,
admiring this amazing beautiful world, in all it's glee,
finding a common ground, a universal language to spree,
a gentle voice guiding like a compass, to take the risk
and see,
to find the inner truth, a quiet bin to free,
feel the stillness of the night, where the sole companion
is me.

In the act of sharing and caring, my heart finds its
delight,
a sense of joy and purpose, that is totally upright,

in the act of forgiveness, my heart finds desired insight,
Letting go of the burdens, and wounds of past fight,
my vision is clear, despite closed eyes, I can now cite,
a heartful presence, that makes me sublime and bright.

Heart that listens deeply, I am now able to hear,
a soft voice that is always near, to tap into, the presence
so dear,
Heartful presence blooms without the onset of spring so
clear,
radiant heart beats, to let the elixir of life overflow in
cheer,
warmth, compassion and gratitude in grace is attained
despite fear,
an assurance that we have arrived, in Heartfulness so
dear!

14. Simplicity

In a world full of clutter, chaos, noise and fray,
with distractions, loud possessions, that clog the way,
no space to pause, taking us away from the roots in
dismay,
letting go of excess attachments, "Nouns" and all
displays,
finding a niche that is genuine, making space for
authentic to stay,
in this turmoil of circumstances, it is difficult to find our
bay.

For improved clarity and attention, learn to unlearn
regularly and know,
to foster innovation and entrepreneurship, to relearn and
glow,
as the purpose is focused to be the flow,
a path that is simple, authentic, free from dismay to
grow,
the pace is secure, sure, deep lasting, yet completely
slow,

this new trend is the confidence, to adopt and show.

The idea is to live intentionally, connect, what truly
matters in life,
Strengthening coping skills, adaptability, and calmness
so fine,
a lifestyle that is simple, honest and humble for
humanity to shine,
the trusted intentions to guide, without pride, and define,
to shed all excuses, excess, and invisible imaginary
guideline,
a life uncomplicated, free from strife, to find the insight
alive,
let's choose Simplicity, a true and authentic skyline!

15. Unknown Unknowns

Within each one of us, there is a quite space so fine,
where the unknown resides, and mysteries entwine,
a place where questions linger, and answers hide,
where the understanding divides, to know what we
decide,
in this new thoughtless state, where knowledge may
update,
the surprises can wait, to challenge our perceptions and
inundate.

In this niche of uncertainties, we must all be bold,
to venture forth, with an open mind and let ideas unfold,
in the unknown unknown's, lies hidden truth untold,
discoveries awaiting, to reshape and mold,
we think we know, but do we really know all that is told,
in this matrix of known unknowns, our understandings
are old.

There are limits to knowledge, beyond which we can't
assign,

to know our limitations, be humble, to acknowledge and
realign,
to recognize that there's still more to learn, to explore
seek and design,
as the key to curiosity lies, in exploring the unknown
sign,
on the wheel of unknown unknowns. where mysteries
align,
to uncover the secret wisdom, in awareness to design .

On boarding the voyage of creativity, venture into the
unknown often,
to discover new wisdom, when the mind soften,
spark that ignites, a flame of enthusiasm foreign,
to guide us through the history, where the curiosity
cautions,
for in this unknown, exists the potential for growth
forgotten,
with new experiences, impressions and relearning
gotten.

With courage venture the unknown chore,
unearth a secret to decode, all that is in store,
this intersection for wisdom to score,
a keenness to discover, go forth and more,
as in the gaps of unknown, lies truth in bore,

a paradox of mysteries and intuitions, hard to ignore,
to explore the wisdom of 'Unknown Unknown's' core.

16. Earth School--A Leaning Place

Welcome to planet earth, a place to wonder in delight,
where souls wander, a quest to explore the secret insight,
In this Universal matrix, all beings aspire for the might,
from birth till death, the energy flows across like knight,
opportunities as challenges, exploring memorable routes
upright,
gliding to discover the resilience, weeding out weakness
in sight.

Earth's gentle embrace, a soothing energy surrounds in
grace,
ancient tree's wisdom, where abundance is to chase,
a jumble of learnings, unlearning and relearning in
phase,
sunlight's enchanting 'Tindal effect', reflecting beyond
space,
this tree of life is grand, truly mine to phrase,
source to connect, as earth and sky meet face to face.

In Indian mythology, the Theme of life is a legend to
behold,
ancient Mesopotamia considers the Tree of life, a supra
threshold,
the Egyptian mythology defines, a connection with
afterlife to uphold,
in modern times, this Tree of Life, invites numerous
stories untold,
it's a reminder of our roots, that reflect the glory of the
past to unfold,
this iconic treasure of life, consists of mysteries new and
old.

It's spiritual significance is divine, for us to seek,
like a bridge between heaven and earthy peak,
in many cultures, the Tree of life is endeared to speak,
as a representative in various forms, a fine mix to creak,
like a soothing melody, the fruits as seeds tweak,
a symbol that is creative, as nourishment from earth's
core creek.

Planet earth our home, to heal the wounds of past,
from pollution to destruction, a future to last,
Learning to live in harmony with Nature's cast,
finding ways to recharge, the damage done so fast,
sustainable living, renewable energy, reducing footprint
chart,

let's join hands in protecting the biosphere reserves and
wildlife to start.

We are all connected in this web of might,
where duality dissolves, to let 'Oneness' ignite,
maintain a delicate balance, as the present rope is tight,
let the active part of this ecosystem delight,
actions today impacts the planet's future plight,
let the web of life intertwine, to be the change all right,
as students on Earth school....A learning place foresight.

17. Wabi Sabi

A World broken, bored, drained, yet set to pace,
the cracks and crevices, torn and old with race ,
in the stillness, where the imperfection and
impermanence trace,
a philosophy to celebrate, where the incomplete and torn
grace,
a bliss that is profound, despite the shortcomings in
place,
is where the magic happens, in this unique space.

The external world is aspiring, to be perfectionist's
delight,
a World that's wounded and worn, yet a perfect score to
fight,
majority of the "Nouns" are broken, they fail, fall to
plight,
a fleeting glimpse of the Universal transient light,
the wholesomeness gives way to incompleteness in
sight,
I can now choose solace, with imperfections might.

Cherish each moment, cracks in the sidewalk base,
an unusual way, to slow, at ease to avoid chase,
a blank state, so dear for a new idea to praise,
a clumsy, wobbly style, a pause, an unusual surface,
the uneven lines, imperfect brush strokes gaze,
imperfections are grand, that exist in deep, dense forest
maze.

This place is of gentle ease, where imperfections hold the
perfect trees,
a fleeting sigh, to slow down and wander like bees,
weathered and old wood, hidden stories in every grain
seize,
the charm of fading light, bounty in brokenness to refine,
snowflake's random fall, each unique, yet a uniform
design,
Wabi Sabi, a conscious choice, to capture the divine.

18. The Global Zen's

Digital World is all around, an evolving global
community no doubt,
Wires, towers, transmitters, signals etc, we hardly bother
about,
creating networks, beyond compare, across the globe, as
digital spout,
to carry our voice, to echo back with a global choice, in
digital shout,
as the differences melt, the similarities flow, as a digital
pout,
a common niche, a community as Global Netizens
sprout.

No doubt the world today is smaller, than ever before,
the global village is where we generate a digital home,
sharing our traditions, cultures, values and more,
breaking the digital barriers, minimizing digital divide
here,
a seamless connectivity to assure, in this digital age dear,
Global Netizens unit in a digital world, where internet

access to all is clear.

Global Citizens of the world align, to let humanity
entwine,
despite programming of different cultures, yet a common
bond so fine,
as 'Doers' and 'Dreamers 'align, to ensure equality, justice
for all to define,
this planet is our home, we as guests, let's join hands to
shine,
as the stewards, of this earth, be mindful and take care of
all alike,
as change makers, let Global Citizens, work for a world
to refine.

As Global Citizens and Global Netzines, we are
connected with the digital crew,
let's strive for unity, to create a future, plugging the
differences, between the two,
Global Citizens are rooted, with a strong community to
renew,
while Global Netizens, are interconnected online all day
anew,
Global Citizens are grounded, hands on within real
world clew,
while Global Netizens, may face virtual tests, online
harassment and digital askew.

Yet there's an intersection, where the two meet and
greet,
a space where online and offline Zen's, come together to
treat,
let the people across the globe, join in the fleet,
to share views and concerns, and establish a robust
retreat,
learn to respect each other's perspectives and visions to
tweet,
the future is a mixed bag of global and digital tools to
sleet.

A dependable niche to share, amongst Citizens and
Netizens alike,
the technology is here, to bridge the gap or divide,
to create a platform, for all to unite, thrive and survive.
let each one be a Global Citizen' and 'Global Netizen' fine
,
creating joy for each other, to maximize and shine,
The Global Zen's create a 'New World Order' to define.

19. Compassion

Beyond the boundaries that divide and differences that
separate,
aspire to focus on a sense of humility, that's profound
and great,
like a soothing balm, for the wounded individual's plight,
a kind ear, that is open to hear our deepest fear in sight,
times when majority around us, are often cold and
arrogant,
a lantern of empathy, guiding 24x7 as new light.

Humility on earth school, flows in many forms, faces so
clear,
from the parents who tends, to the siblings so dear,
from the teachers who genuinely guide, to the friend
who listen and care,
from the volunteer who serves, to the strangers who
dare,
the charity that assures, for those in need and in pain,
the activist that fights, for justice and human rights to
gain,

the sensitivity that glows in the eyes, overtaking all
sufferings and blame.

A gesture that reduces stress and anxiety, aligning to the
peace inside,
abundant empathy, understanding, fostering humanity's
pride,
creating a ripple effect, spreading kindness all way to
guide,
as an easy everyday practice, to work on and adopt at
time,
be the torch bearer, the game changer, leaving
meaningful footprints behind,
Compassion to adopt, is important to survive.

Choose to be the light in the darkness, a hope in despair,
be the universal love to heal and share,
gratitude as linked value, a guiding light to spare,
Compassion is the virtue, that is a profound prayer,
empathy's gentle touch, calms the mind to repair,
kindness like rain, nourishes heart's deep listening with
care,
embracing all insecurities, accepting Compassion to dare.

20. Stillness awaits

Situations in external environment are loud, restless to
face,
Learn to pause, zero the thoughts, slow down in race,
a quiet refuge to turn around, in the exclusive space,
carved in a gentle tone, appears as special place,
to align and focus, anytime, anywhere, in sacred grace,
a sense of purpose guiding effortlessly, through the
darkest phase.

Admiring the natural beauty, overlooked and unseen,
a silent elegance, woven into the fabric of life to lean,
the deep silence of the forest, in serenity with
mountain's sheen,
majestic in every form, this safe adobe to admire the
green,
the awe-inspiring presence, inviting to explore the preen,
this new route takes me to the world so pristine.

Stillness as a practice, takes time and patience to refine,
Self-acclaimed discipline, cultivates a new task across

rough line,
this profound, simple awareness present around to
define,
the feeling of oneness, where duality dissolves in time,
a sense of belonging, in this amazing shrine,
a treasure so precious to absorb, breathe and confine.

A sense of contentment, that's always in reach to adore,
a blessing always in store, a language that is prime to
explore,
a sense of stillness, power to mend all what truly is
before,
morning's gentle hush, settles with silent starry nights
offshore,
a gentle voice that whispers, as stillness attracts to
implore,
Universe is vast and mysterious, where stillness awaits
galore.

21. Life a Marathon

The pace of life a rhythm, at times steady, a unique
stride,
we stumble and fall, dust ourselves off, to never give up
the side,
adapting to twists and turns, pushing our limits, we
realize,
to discover the might, we never had in our mind to
visualize,
we share laughter and fears, with strangers and
companions alike,
learning from the unpleasant experiences, to grow wise
and rise,
maintain the pace, at times fast or slow, to conserve the
energy inside,
as running a marathon requires, a will to reach the finish
line.

Running the race of life with pride and cheer, along with
joys and tears,
Life like marathon is about participating, observing near,

different phases generate, a mixed bag of emotions to
fear,
a sense of accomplishment, admiring, looking back here,
we have travelled far and wide, collected memories so
dear,
Knowing life is a marathon, that's full of learnings to
cheer.

In the life's roller coaster journey, we find two types of
runners to describe,
marathon runners or sprinters with their own unique
tribe,
the marathon runners with endurance, a steady
consistent sight,
the sprinters with speed and agility, dash and dart to
delight,
marathon mindset is of patience, knowing that the
journey is long,
a steady, consistent stride, as slow and steady win's the
prize.
not swayed by instant gratification, to ensure a steady
claim,
nor driven by adrenaline, speed and intensity, as the goal
is beyond aim,
neither quick to react nor fast to respond, driven by
purpose, a mission to claim.

The mindset is different with patience and impatience to
sear,
with perseverance, persistence and endurance loud and
clear,
despite significant differences, there are similarities to
bear,
driven by desire to complete, in the passionate gear,
physical strength in coherence with mental balance,
overtakes all fear,
the human race is about running, either a marathon or a
sprint dear.

Reliving every moment, every step gone bye with pride,
to acknowledge our victories, overtake the challengs on
side,
to find life's a marathon, full of lessons to repeat and
refine,
a journey long and wide, give all we've got, with every
step to glide,
a test of endurance, a challenge to face the steady slide,
creating 'Life as a Marathon', greatest achievement to
abide!

www.ingramcontent.com/pod-product-compliance
Lightning Source LLC
La Vergne TN
LVHW050936200726
843508LV00011B/2357